enVision™ Algebra 1
Assessment Readiness Workbook

Pearson

Boston, Massachusetts

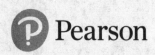

ISBN-13: 978-0-328-93169-9
ISBN-10:   0-328-93169-1

Contents

enVision Algebra 1

Standards Practice Week 1

Selected Response

1. A sporting complex charges $6 to use its facility. The expression $0.25b + 6$ models the total cost to hit b baseballs in the batting cages. What is the cost per baseball?

   (A) $6.25

   (B) $6.00

   (C) $0.25

   (D) $0.19

Constructed Response

2. The sum of the angle measures of a triangle is 180°. Find the measure of each angle.

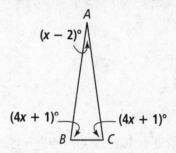

   $m\angle A$ _____ $m\angle B$ ___ $m\angle C$ ___

Extended Response

3. A student stated that the sum of two real numbers is always a rational number. Is the student correct? Explain why or why not and provide an example to support your answer.

Standards Practice Week 2

Selected Response

1. Which equation represents the following sentence?

The sum of a number p and 12 is 34.

Ⓐ $p - 12 = 34$

Ⓑ $12p = 34$

Ⓒ $p + 12 = 34$

Ⓓ $p + 34 = 12$

2. What is the solution of $-27 = \frac{m}{9}$?

Ⓐ -243 Ⓒ 3

Ⓑ -3 Ⓓ 243

Constructed Response

3. An architect builds a scale model of a skyscraper for a land development proposal. The model is 2 ft tall. The scale of the model is 1 in. : 7.2 m.

How tall is the proposed skyscraper in meters? Show your work.

Extended Response

4. Write the correct explanation next to each step.

- Distributive Property
- Simplify using addition.
- Add 9 to each side and simplify.
- Use multiplication to simplify.
- Multiply each side by $-\frac{4}{3}$ and simplify.

Steps	Explanation
$-\frac{3}{4}(x + 4) - 6 = 54$	Original equation
$-\frac{3}{4}(x) - \frac{3}{4}(4) - 6 = 54$	
$-\frac{3}{4}(x) + (-3) - 6 = 54$	
$-\frac{3}{4}(x) - 9 = 54$	
$-\frac{3}{4}(x) = 63$	
$x = -84$	

Standards Practice Week 3

Selected Response

1. Tamika is buying snacks. She buys 6 apples and a juice. The juice costs $1.25. The total cost is $5.75. How much is 1 apple?

Ⓐ $0.50

Ⓑ $.75

Ⓒ $1.00

Ⓓ $0.25

Constructed Response

2. You can find the net force F on an object by using the formula $F = ma$, where m is the mass of the object in kilograms and a is its acceleration in meters per second squared. What is the mass of an object that has a net force of 72 kg m/s² and an acceleration of 6 m/s²?

Extended Response

3. A T-shirt maker wants to open his first store. If he chooses the store on Main Street, he will pay $650 in rent and will charge $32 per T-shirt. If he chooses the store on Broad Street, he will pay $440 in rent and will charge $26 per T-shirt. How many T-shirts would he have to sell in one month to make the same profit at either location?

a. Write an equation to solve the problem.

b. Solve the equation you wrote in part (a) to answer the question.

Standards Practice Week 4

Selected Response

1. Solve $-2x \geq -18$.

   Ⓐ $x \geq -9$

   Ⓑ $x \geq 9$

   Ⓒ $x \leq 9$

   Ⓓ $x \leq -16$

2. Which ordered pair is a solution to the equation $y = 3x + 6$?

   Ⓐ $(3, 1)$

   Ⓑ $(-3, 3)$

   Ⓒ $(0, 6)$

   Ⓓ $(6, 0)$

Constructed Response

3. The function rule $h(x) = 2x + 6$ represents the height h, in centimeters, of a plant after x weeks of growth.

   Graph the function. If the plant continues to grow at the same rate, how tall will it be after 9 weeks?

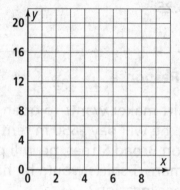

Extended Response

4. Consider the ordered pairs $(0, 40)$, $(1, 45)$, $(2, 50)$, $(3, 55)$, $(4, 60)$, and $(5, 65)$.

   a. Represent the ordered pairs as a table.

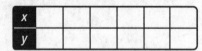

   b. Represent the ordered pairs as an equation.

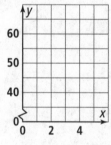

   c. Represent the ordered pairs and the equation as a graph.

   d. Describe a situation that the ordered pairs might represent.

Standards Practice Week 5

Selected Response

1. Which equation represents the data in the table?

Number of Hours Worked, h	Number of Paint Cans Remaining, p
0	12
1	10
2	8
3	6

Ⓐ $p = 12h - 2$

Ⓑ $p = 2h - 12$

Ⓒ $p = 12 - 2h$

Ⓓ $p = 2 - 12h$

2. Which is an equation of a line in point-slope form that has slope 9 and passes through $(-3, 6)$?

Ⓐ $y - 6 = 9(x + 3)$

Ⓑ $y - 6 = 9(x - 3)$

Ⓒ $y + 3 = 9(x - 6)$

Ⓓ $y - 6 = -3(x - 9)$

Constructed Response

3. Sage earns $6 per hour doing chores.

a. Make a table and write an equation to show the relationship between the number of hours worked h and the wages earned w.

Hours	Wages

b. How many hours will Sage need to work to earn $30?

Extended Response

4. A department store advertises a sale where the customer chooses the discount. A customer may choose a flat discount of $20 off any purchase or 20% off the total purchase price. The final purchase price of an item was $175.

a. What are the possible prices of the item before each discount?

b. Which discount represents a bigger savings in cost for the customer?

Name _____

Standards Practice Week 6

Selected Response

1. Which of the following is NOT a function?

Ⓐ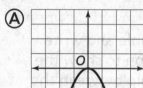

Ⓒ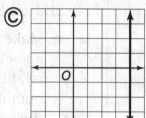

Ⓑ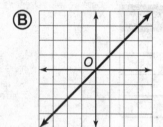

Ⓓ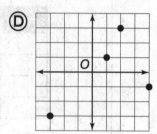

Constructed Response

2. **a.** Draw a line on the graph below that has the same slope as the line drawn and that passes through (−2, 1).

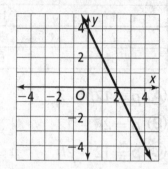

b. What is an equation of the line you drew?

Extended Response

3. Refer to the graph at the right. Write each equation in the correct column.

- $y - 2 = \frac{1}{2}(x - 4)$
- $y - 4 = \frac{1}{2}(x - 2)$
- $y - 1 = \frac{1}{2}(x + 4)$
- $y + 4 = 2(x - 1)$
- $y - 1 = 2(x + 4)$

Possible Equation of the Line Drawn	NOT an Equation of the Line Drawn

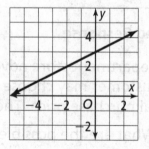

Standards Practice Week 7

Selected Response

1. Find the slope of the line that passes through the points $(-1, 9)$ and $(3, 17)$.

   Ⓐ -8

   Ⓑ -2

   Ⓒ 2

   Ⓓ 8

Constructed Response

2. What is the value of the expression $4(xy)^2 - 2x + 5y$ for $x = 6$ and $y = 2$?

Extended Response

3. Camilla and Nadia start a business tutoring students in math. They rent an office for $250 per month and charge $20 per hour per student.

   a. If they have 10 students each for one hour per week, how much profit do they make in a month? Write a linear equation to solve this problem. Assume that there are 4 weeks in one month.

   b. Graph the equation from part (a) and explain what it models.

enVision Algebra 1
PearsonRealize.com

Standards Practice Week 8

Selected Response

1. What is the recursive formula for the sequence 2, 24, 46, 68, 90, . . . ?

   (A) $a_1 = 2; a_n = a_{n-1} + 22$

   (B) $a_1 = 2; a_n = a_{n-1} - 22$

   (C) $a_1 = 2; a_n = a_{n+1} + 22$

   (D) $a_1 = 2; a_n = a_{n+1} - 22$

Constructed Response

2. The sequence $\frac{1}{2}$, $1\frac{1}{4}$, 2, $2\frac{3}{4}$, $3\frac{1}{2}$ is an arithmetic sequence.

   a. Write an explicit formula for the sequence.

   b. Find the value of the 12th term of the sequence.

Extended Response

3. Stacy opens a savings account with a deposit of $150. She deposits an additional $20 every week after that.

   a. Write an explicit function and a recursive function to represent this situation.

   b. Choose a function from part (a) and determine how much money will be in the account after 12 weeks if Stacy makes no additional deposits or withdrawals.

   c. Explain why you chose the function you used in part (b).

Name _____

Standards Practice Week 9

Selected Response

1. Solve the formula $pV = nRT$ for T.

   (A) $T = pV - nR$

   (B) $T = pVnR$

   (C) $T = \dfrac{pV}{nR}$

   (D) $T = pV$

Constructed Response

2. The ordered pairs below show (study time in hours, test score) for a group of students. Make a scatter plot and draw a trend line for the data. What would you expect a student who studied 6 hours to score on the test?

   (3, 72), (5, 80), (2, 65), (7, 90), (1, 62), (4, 70), (8, 92)

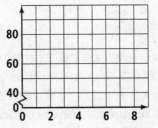

Extended Response

3. A teacher surveys her students about the amount of physical activity they get each week. She also measures each student's body mass index (BMI).

Active Hours	10	4	5	7	10	9	7
BMI	16	26	23	20	15	17	18

   a. Use a calculator to find the correlation coefficient for the data.

   b. Does this relationship show correlation or causation or both? Explain.

Standards Practice Week 10

Selected Response

1. What is the solution to the following system of equations?

$$5y - 3x = 14$$
$$y + 3x = 10$$

Ⓐ (2, 4)

Ⓑ (4, 2)

Ⓒ (−2, −4)

Ⓓ (2, −4)

Constructed Response

2. Solve the following system of equations by using elimination. Show your work.

$$x + 4y = 6$$
$$3x - 4y = 14$$

Extended Response

3. Alejandro loves to go to the movies. He goes both at night and during the day. The cost of a matinee is $7. The cost of an evening show is $12. Alejandro went to see a total of 6 movies and spent $52. Let x represent the number of matinee movies attended and y represent the number of evening show movies attended.

a. How many of each type of movie did he attend? Write a system of equations and solve by graphing.

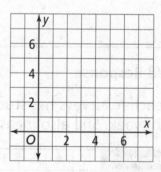

b. Why is the intersection of the graphs of the linear equations the solution?

Standards Practice Week 11

Selected Response

1. Which ordered pair is NOT a solution of $y > 5x + 3$?

    (A) (2, 14)

    (B) (1, 8)

    (C) (−1, 2)

    (D) (0, 4)

Constructed Response

2. Graph $4x + 2y > 8$

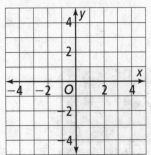

Extended Response

3. The Cougars scored a total of 84 points in their basketball game last night against the Bears. The Cougars made no one-point shots, and a total of 38 two-point and three-point shots. Let x represent the number of two-point shots and y represent the number of three-point shots.

    a. How many two-point shots did the Cougars make? How many three-point shots did the Cougars make? Write and solve a system of equations that can be used to solve this problem.

    b. Graph the system of equations.

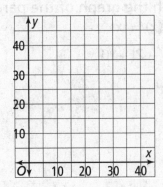

Name _____

Standards Practice Week 12

Selected Response

1. Which is the graph of the solution for the system of inequalities?

   $y > -x + 2$

   $y < x + 4$

Ⓐ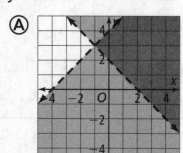

Ⓒ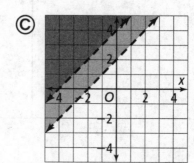

Ⓑ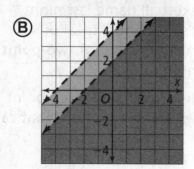

Ⓓ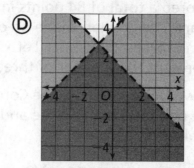

Constructed Response

2. Compare the graph of function g below with the graph of the parent function $f(x) = |x|$.

   $g(x) = \frac{1}{3}|x - 2| + 10$

Extended Response

3. Manuel wants to raise between $250 and $350 for charity. His parents donated $70. Manuel plans to ask others to contribute $10 each. How many people will need to contribute for Manuel to reach his goal?

   a. Write an inequality to solve the problem.

   b. Show your solution as a graph and explain your solution in words.

Standards Practice Week 13

Selected Response

1. Solve for *x*.

   $$\frac{x}{3} = \frac{10}{15}$$

   Ⓐ 2

   Ⓑ 3

   Ⓒ 12

   Ⓓ 15

Constructed Response

2. Graph the function.

   $$f(x) = \begin{cases} 1 - 0.5x, & x < 1 \\ x, & x \geq 1 \end{cases}$$

   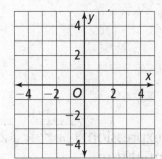

Extended Response

3. The length of a rectangle is 4 more than twice its width. If the perimeter of the rectangle can be no more than 92 ft, what are all of the possible widths of the rectangle?

   a. Write an inequality to solve the problem.

   b. Show your solution as a graph and describe the solution in words.

   <————+——+——+——+——+——+——+——+——+——+——+——+————>

Standards Practice Week 14

Selected Response

1. What is the simplified form of $6^{-2}x^3y^{-5}$?

   Ⓐ $-12x^35y$

   Ⓑ $-36x^3y$

   Ⓒ $\dfrac{x^3}{36y^5}$

   Ⓓ $\dfrac{x^3}{12y^5}$

2. Write the expression $\sqrt[3]{5at^4} \times \sqrt[3]{25a^2}$ in exponential form.

   Ⓐ $5^{\frac{1}{3}}at^2$

   Ⓑ $5^{\frac{2}{3}}a^{\frac{1}{3}}t^{\frac{4}{3}}$

   Ⓒ $5at^{\frac{4}{3}}$

   Ⓓ $125a^3t^4$

Constructed Response

3. Simplify the expression $\left(4g^{\frac{1}{3}} \cdot 2h^{\frac{3}{5}}\right)\left(3g^{\frac{2}{3}} \cdot h^{\frac{1}{5}}\right)$. Show your work.

Extended Response

4. Your classmate writes that for $b > 0$, $b^{-(xy)} = \dfrac{1}{(b^x)^y}$ for all real numbers x and y.

   Is your classmate correct? Explain how you know and show examples to justify your explanation.

Name _____

Standards Practice Week 15

Selected Response

1. Which is a recursive definition for the following geometric sequence?

$$4, 16, 64, 256, \ldots$$

Ⓐ $a_1 = 0$; $a_n = 4(a_{n-1})$

Ⓑ $a_1 = 4$; $a_n = 4(a_{n-1})$

Ⓒ $a_1 = 4$; $a_n = 4 + a_{n-1}$

Ⓓ $a_1 = 0$; $a_n = 4 + a_{n-1}$

Constructed Response

2. A population of lizards in a large region doubles every year. The number of lizards can be modeled by the equation $y = 500 \cdot 2^x$, where x is the number of years after a researcher measures the population size. When $x = -3$, what does the value of y represent?

Extended Response

3. There are 6 mice in an attic. Their population is growing at a rate of 12% per month.

   a. Write an exponential growth function to model this situation.

   b. How many mice will there be in the attic in two years if nothing is done to slow down or stop the growth?

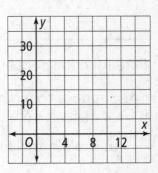

   c. Sketch a graph of the function.

Standards Practice Week 16

Selected Response

1. How many terms are in the expression $5n^6 - n^4 - 3n^2 - 2n + 4$?

   Ⓐ 3   Ⓒ 5

   Ⓑ 4   Ⓓ 7

2. What is the degree of the monomial $4a^5bc$?

   Ⓐ 4

   Ⓑ 5

   Ⓒ 6

   Ⓓ 7

Constructed Response

3. On the first day of an experiment there were 8 bacteria in a petri dish. On the second day there were 16. On the third day there were 32 and so on.

   a. Write an explicit formula and recursive formula for the number of bacteria after n days.

   b. Interpret the parts of the formula and explain their meaning within the context of this situation.

Extended Response

4. Suppose that a new house is worth $250,000 and that it depreciates at a rate of 16% a year.

   a. Explain this situation in terms of growth or decay.

   b. Write a function to model this situation.

   c. Estimate the value of the house after 5 years.

Name _____

Standards Practice Week 17

Selected Response

1. Which expression is equivalent to $(x - 3)^2$?

   Ⓐ $2x - 6$

   Ⓑ $x^2 + 9$

   Ⓒ $x^2 - 6x + 9$

   Ⓓ $x^2 - 9x - 6$

Constructed Response

2. Classify each expression as equivalent to $3x^2 + 14x$ or NOT equivalent to $3x^2 + 14x$. Write each expression inside the appropriate box below.

   $(5x^2 + 10x + 6) - (2x^2 - 4x + 6)$

   $x(3x + 14)$

   $6x^2 - (9x^2 + 12x) - 2x$

   $(x^2 + 6x^2) + (-4x^2 + 2x - 4x + 16x)$

Expressions Equivalent to $3x^2 + 14x$	Expressions Not Equivalent to $3x^2 + 14x$

Extended Response

3. The length of a rectangular sandbox is $4x + 1$. The width of the sandbox is $x - 2$.

   a. What polynomial in standard form represents the area of the sandbox?

   b. Name the polynomial based on its degree and number of terms.

Standards Practice Week 18

Selected Response

1. Factor the following polynomial.

   $5x^2 + 27x - 18$

   (A) $(5x + 3)(x + 6)$

   (B) $(5x - 2)(x - 9)$

   (C) $(5x - 3)(x + 6)$

   (D) $(5x + 2)(x - 9)$

Constructed Response

2. **a.** Simplify the expression $(x - 3)^3$.

   b. Name the polynomial based on its degree.

Extended Response

3. Refer to the figure shown. When necessary, use 3.14 for π.

   a. What is an expression in standard form for the area of the rectangle? Simplify your answer.

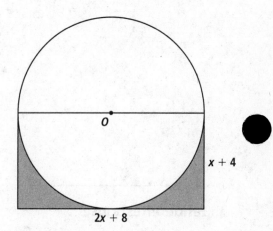

$x + 4$

$2x + 8$

   b. What is an expression in standard form for the area of the circle? Simplify your answer.

   c. What is an expression in standard form for the area of the shaded region? Simplify your answer.

Standards Practice Week 19

Selected Response

1. Factor the following polynomial.

    $4x^2 - 31x - 8$

    Ⓐ $(4x + 1)(x - 8)$

    Ⓑ $(4x - 2)(2x + 4)$

    Ⓒ $(4x + 4)(x - 2)$

    Ⓓ $(4x - 1)(x + 8)$

Constructed Response

2. The area of a square window is $64x^2 + 96x + 36$. What is an expression for the side length of the window?

Extended Response

3. A rectangular garden measuring 8 m by 12 m is to have a pathway x meters wide installed around its perimeter. The area of the pathway will be equal to the area of the garden.

    a. Make a sketch of this situation and write a polynomial in standard form to model the total area of the garden and pathway. Explain your work.

    b. What will be the width of the pathway?

Standards Practice Week 20

Selected Response

1. What is the vertex of the parabola with equation $y = 4x^2 + 3$?

   Ⓐ (3, 4)

   Ⓑ (4, 3)

   Ⓒ (3, 0)

   Ⓓ (0, 3)

Constructed Response

2. **a.** Graph the equation $y = 2x^2 - 8$.

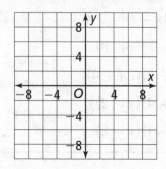

   b. Find the solutions to $2x^2 - 8 = 0$.

Extended Response

3. You throw a ball into the air from a deck. The ball's height h, in feet, after t seconds can be modeled by the function $h(t) = -16t^2 + 16t + 12$.

   a. After how many seconds will the ball hit the ground? Solve by factoring and by sketching a graph.

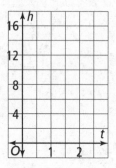

   b. Interpret the key features of the graph and how they relate to this situation.

Standards Practice Week 21

Selected Response

1. Choose all the solutions of
$x^2 - 10 = -3x$.

   Ⓐ $x = -5$

   Ⓑ $x = -2$

   Ⓒ $x = 5$

   Ⓓ $x = 2$

Constructed Response

2. Solve $6x^2 + 4 = -11x$.
Show your work.

Extended Response

3. a. Solve the equation $x^2 - 5x = 6$.

   b. Explain how the solutions you found in part (a) help
   you to graph $y = x^2 - 5x - 6$.

   c. Sketch a graph of the function.

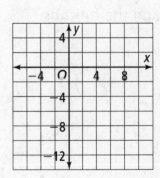

Standards Practice Week 22

Selected Response

1. What is the vertex of the parabola with equation $y = x^2 - 2$?

    Ⓐ $(0, -2)$

    Ⓑ $(2, 0)$

    Ⓒ $(1, -2)$

    Ⓓ $(-2, 1)$

Constructed Response

2. Graph a line that has an x-intercept of 4 and a y-intercept of 3.

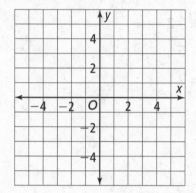

Extended Response

3. a. Given $f(x) = -3x^2 - 5x + 8$. Find all of the solutions of $f(x) = 0$ by factoring.

    b. Explain how to use your solutions from part (a) to graph f.

    c. Graph the function.

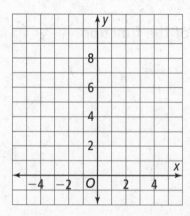

Name _____

Standards Practice Week 23

Selected Response

1. What is the simplified form of
   $7\sqrt{18} + 4\sqrt{2}$?

   Ⓐ $5\sqrt{2}$

   Ⓑ $25\sqrt{2}$

   Ⓒ $11\sqrt{6}$

   Ⓓ $11\sqrt{20}$

Constructed Response

2. a. Solve $x^2 + 6x = -2$ by completing the square.

   b. Use the zeros you found in part (a) to graph the function defined by the polynomial equation $x^2 + 6x = y - 2$.

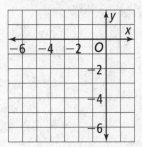

Extended Response

3. The area of a rooftop can be expressed as $9x^2 - 6x + 1$. The rooftop is a rectangle with side lengths that are factors of the polynomial describing its area.

   a. What expression describes the length of one side of the rooftop?

   b. What type of rectangle is the rooftop? How do you know?

   c. If the area of the rooftop is 529 m², what is x?

Standards Practice Week 24

Selected Response

1. Solve $x^2 + 30x = -30$ by completing the square.

 Ⓐ $x = -15 \pm \sqrt{195}$

 Ⓑ $x = 15 \pm \sqrt{195}$

 Ⓒ $x = -15 \pm \sqrt{255}$

 Ⓓ $x = 15 \pm \sqrt{255}$

Constructed Response

2. **a.** Solve $2x^2 + 8x = -3$ by completing the square.

 b. Use the zeros you found in part (a) to graph the function defined by the polynomial equation $2x^2 + 8x = y - 3$.

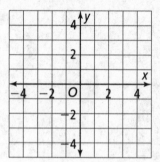

Extended Response

3. The area of a rooftop can be expressed as $16x^2 + 24x + 9$. The rooftop is a rectangle with side lengths that are factors of the polynomial describing its area.

 a. What expression describes the length of one side of the rooftop?

 b. What type of rectangle is the rooftop? How do you know?

 c. If the area of the rooftop is 961 m², what is x?

Standards Practice Week 25

Selected Response

1. Solve $x^2 + 4x - 20 = 12$ by using the quadratic formula.

   (A) $x = 2, 16$

   (B) $x = -2, 16$

   (C) $x = -8, -20$

   (D) $x = 4, -8$

Constructed Response

2. The flight path of a bird is modeled by the function $y = x^2 - 10x + 15$, where y is the bird's height in centimeters above the water and x is time in seconds.

   a. Find the roots of the equation by completing the square. Show your work. Write your answer to the nearest hundredth.

   b. What does this solution tell you about the bird's flight?

Extended Response

3. You can use the formula $V = \ell w h$ to find the volume of a box.

   a. Write a quadratic equation in standard form that represents the volume of the box.

   b. The volume of the box is 30 ft^3. Solve the quadratic equation for x.

   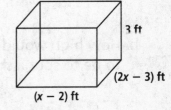

   c. Use the solution from part (b) to find the length and width of the box. Describe any extraneous solutions.

Standards Practice Week 26

Selected Response

1. What is the value of x?

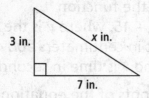

3 in. x in.

7 in.

Ⓐ $x = \sqrt{58}$

Ⓑ $x = 3\sqrt{6}$

Ⓒ $x = 2\sqrt{10}$

Ⓓ $x = 2\sqrt{5}$

Constructed Response

2. a. Graph the function $y = \sqrt{x + 6} - 1$.

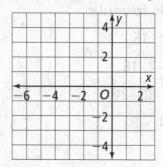

b. What are the domain and range of the function?

Extended Response

3. The distance d, in miles, a person can see through a particular submarine periscope is given by the equation $d = 5\sqrt{h - 4} + 4$, where h is the height in feet above water.

a. Graph the equation.

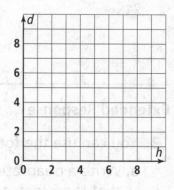

b. How high would the submarine periscope have to be to spot a ship 14 mi away?

Name _____

Standards Practice Week 27

Selected Response

1. Which steps transform the graph of $y = |x|$ into the graph of $y = |x + 2| - 7$?

   Ⓐ Translate 2 units left and 7 units up.

   Ⓑ Translate 2 units right and 7 units up.

   Ⓒ Translate 2 units left and 7 units down.

   Ⓓ Translate 2 units right and 7 units down.

Constructed Response

2. Graph the function $f(x) = \sqrt{x - 4} + 2$.

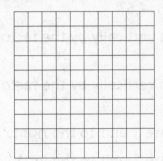

Extended Response

3. **a.** Simplify the expression $\sqrt{9x + 117} - 2$.

   b. Use the result from part (a) to graph the function $f(x) = \sqrt{9x + 117} - 2$ and its parent function in the same coordinate plane.

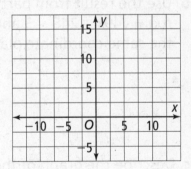

   c. Describe the graph of the function in relation to the graph of its parent function.

Standards Practice Week 28

Selected Response

1. Which steps transform the graph of $y = \sqrt{x}$ into the graph of $y = \frac{1}{2}\sqrt{x-1} + 5$?

Ⓐ Stretch vertically by the factor of 2.

Ⓑ Stretch vertically by the factor of $\frac{1}{2}$.

Ⓒ Translate 1 unit to the right.

Ⓓ Translate 1 unit to the left.

Ⓔ Translate 5 units up.

Ⓕ Translate 5 units down.

Constructed Response

2. Graph the function $f(x) = \sqrt{x+6} + 6$.

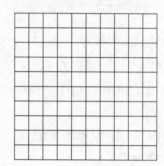

Extended Response

3. **a.** Simplify the expression $\sqrt{49x + 245} - 3$.

b. Use the result from part (a) to graph the function $f(x) = \sqrt{49x + 245} - 3$ and its parent function in the same coordinate plane.

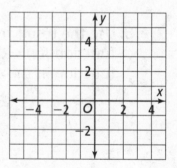

c. Describe the graph of the function in relation to the graph of its parent function.

Name _____

Standards Practice Week 29

Selected Response

1. Which histogram is symmetrical?

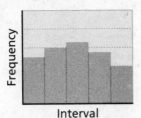

Ⓐ

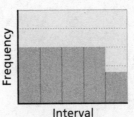

Ⓒ

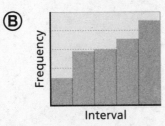

Ⓑ

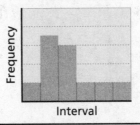

Ⓓ

Constructed Response

2. The hours that a school band practiced per week are listed below.

   8 4 10 6 5 5 9 9 6 6 9 8 4 11 16 12 9

   a. What are the mean, median, mode, and range of the practice times?

   b. Which measure of central tendency best describes the practice times? Justify your answer.

Extended Response

3. The table below shows a company's automobile sales for the first two quarters of the year.

Quarter	Mini Buggy	Overhaul 4 × 4
1	104	288
2	264	150

Calculate the ratio and percent for each of the following situations.

a. Mini Buggy sales in Quarter 1 to all Mini Buggy sales in the first two quarters

b. Mini Buggy sales in Quarter 1 to Mini Buggy sales in Quarter 2

c. Overhaul 4 × 4 sales in Quarter 2 to all Overhaul 4 × 4 sales in the first two quarters

d. Overhaul 4 × 4 sales in Quarter 1 to all automobile sales in both quarters

Name _____

Standards Practice Week 30

Selected Response

1. Which histogram is skewed left?

Ⓐ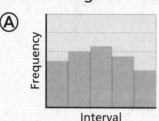

Ⓒ

Ⓑ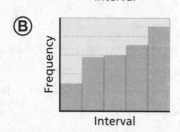

Ⓓ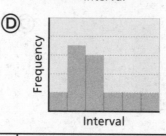

Constructed Response

2. The hours that a babysitter worked per week are listed below.

2 5 5 2 2 4 4 3 2 4 3 16 3

a. What are the mean, median, mode, and range of the number of hours worked?

b. Which measure of central tendency best describes the number of hours worked? Justify your answer.

Extended Response

3. The table below shows a bakery's bread sales for the first two months of the year.

	White	Wheat
January	252	204
February	300	160

Calculate the ratio and percent for each of the following situations.

a. White bread sales in January to all white bread sales in the first two months

b. White bread sales in January to white bread sales in February

c. Wheat bread sales in February to all wheat bread sales in the first two months

Name _____

Practice Test Form A

Part I: Calculator NOT Permitted

1. Which of the following are irrational numbers? Select all that apply.
   - (A) $\frac{3}{4}$
   - (B) $\sqrt{9}$
   - (C) $\sqrt{12}$
   - (D) -9
   - (E) $\sqrt{20}$

2. Rewrite $\frac{(7)^{-5}(2)^5}{(7)^4(2)^{-2}}$ using positive exponents.
   - (A) $\frac{7^{11}}{2^7}$
   - (B) $\frac{7^9}{2^3}$
   - (C) $\frac{2^7}{7^9}$
   - (D) $\frac{2^3}{7^1}$

3. What is the solution to the equation $|2x - 4| + 2 = 16$? Select all that apply.
   - (A) -5
   - (B) -4
   - (C) -2
   - (D) 5
   - (E) 9

4. Which equation represents a line perpendicular to the line that passes through the points $(1, 0)$ and $(3, -4)$?
   - (A) $y = -2x + 2$
   - (B) $y = -\frac{1}{2}x + 2$
   - (C) $y = 2x + 2$
   - (D) $y = \frac{1}{2}x + 2$

5. Maxwell works part-time to earn money for a trip. The amount he saves after working x hours is given by the equation $y = 9.5x + 25$. How much does Maxwell earn per hour?

6. Simplify $(3x^4y^2)^3$.
   - (A) $3x^7y^5$
   - (B) $3x^2y$
   - (C) $9x^{12}y^6$
   - (D) $27x^{12}y^6$

7. Identify the piecewise-defined function that has the same graph as the function $f(x) = |2x - 3|$.

Ⓐ $g(x) = \begin{cases} 2x - 3, & \text{if } x \geq 0 \\ -2x + 3, & \text{if } x < 0 \end{cases}$

Ⓑ $g(x) = \begin{cases} -2x + 3, & \text{if } x \geq \frac{2}{3} \\ 2x - 3, & \text{if } x < \frac{2}{3} \end{cases}$

Ⓒ $g(x) = \begin{cases} 2x - 3, & \text{if } x \geq \frac{3}{2} \\ -2x + 3, & \text{if } x < \frac{3}{2} \end{cases}$

Ⓓ $g(x) = \begin{cases} 2x - 3, & \text{if } x \geq 0 \\ 2x + 3, & \text{if } x < 0 \end{cases}$

8. What type of function is $f(x) = 2x + 5$?

Ⓐ exponential

Ⓑ linear

Ⓒ quadratic

Ⓓ none of the above

9. A student has scores of 88, 97, 89, and 78 on the first four tests in one class. What score must the student earn on the fifth test in order to have an average score of 90?

10. What is an equation for the graph?

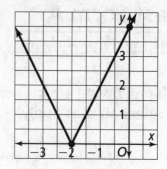

Ⓐ $y = -|2x + 4|$

Ⓑ $y = |2x + 4|$

Ⓒ $y = |2x| + 4$

Ⓓ $y = 2|x + 4|$

11. Which of the following is the best estimate of an equation of a line of best fit for the scatter plot below?

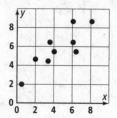

Ⓐ $y = x + 3$

Ⓑ $y = -x + 3$

Ⓒ $y = x + 2$

Ⓓ $y = -x + 2$

12. Arrange the numbers in order from least to greatest.

$$\frac{1}{2}, \sqrt{7}, -\sqrt{2}, -2, \frac{3}{4}, 3$$

Short Response

13. Find the mean and median for the data shown in the dot plot to the nearest hundredth. Explain why they are different.

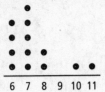

14. The area of a rectangle is $6x^2 + 8x + 2$. The length of the rectangle is $3x + 1$. What is the width?

15. Graph the inequality $2x + 3y > 12$.

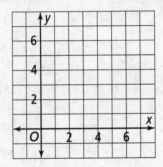

16. Graph the function $f(x) = x^2 + 2x + 1$.

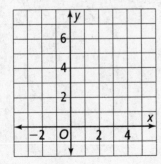

Extended Response

17. A ball is thrown directly upward from a height of 10 ft with an initial velocity of 32 ft/s. The equation $h = -16t^2 + 32t + 10$ gives the height h, in feet, after t seconds.

Part A

How long does it take for the ball to reach its maximum height? Show or explain your work.

Part B

What is the maximum height of the ball? Show or explain your work.

18. Refer to the table below.

x	1	1.5	2	2.5	3	3.5	4
y	7	6.5	6	4.5	2.5	2	1

Part A

Make a scatter plot of the data.

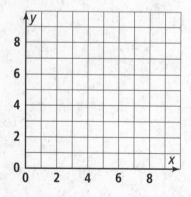

Part B

Estimate an equation of the line of best fit.

Practice Test Form A

Part II: Calculator Permitted

19. The length of the hypotenuse of a right triangle is 39 in. One of the legs measures 15 in. What is the length of the other leg?

  (A) 24 in.

  (B) 27 in.

  (C) 36 in.

  (D) 42 in.

20. Use the Quadratic Formula to solve the equation $2x^2 + 7x - 2 = 3$. Which of the following are solutions of the equation to the nearest hundredth? Select all that apply.

  (A) −4.11

  (B) −3.77

  (C) −3.35

  (D) −0.15

  (E) 0.61

  (F) 2.67

21. How can you describe the graph of $y = 5x + 2$ as a transformation of the graph of $y = 5x$?

  (A) translation 2 units down

  (B) translation 2 units up

  (C) translation 2 units left

  (D) translation 2 units right

22. Graph the solution to the inequality $-2x + 2 \le 8$.

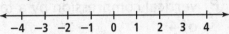

23. Which function does the table represent?

x	−2	−1	0	1	2
y	1	2	3	4	5

  (A) $y = 3x$

  (B) $y = -3x$

  (C) $y = x + 3$

  (D) $y = -x + 3$

24. You deposit $220 in an account that pays 3% interest compounded quarterly. Use the formula $A = P\left(1 + \frac{r}{n}\right)^{nt}$ to determine how much you will have in the account after 5 years.

25. Which of the following describes the graph of the function $y = 4\sqrt[3]{x}$ as a transformation of the graph of the parent function $y = \sqrt[3]{x}$?

Ⓐ translation 4 units up

Ⓑ vertical compression by a factor of 4

Ⓒ vertical stretch by a factor of 4

Ⓓ reflection across the line with equation $y = 4$

26. What is the solution of the system?

$y = 4x + 1$
$y = 3x + 5$

27. Which of the following is an equation for the transformation of the graph of the parent function $y = \sqrt{x}$ shown below?

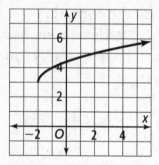

Ⓐ $y = \sqrt{x + 3} - 2$

Ⓑ $y = \sqrt{x - 2} + 3$

Ⓒ $y = \sqrt{x - 3} + 2$

Ⓓ $y = \sqrt{x + 2} + 3$

28. The formula for the volume of a cylinder in cubic feet is $V = \pi r^2 h$, where r is the radius of the base, in feet, and h is the height, in feet. A cylinder has volume 320π ft^3. Its height is 20 ft. What is its diameter?

29. Students in 9th and 10th grade were asked whether they preferred to listen to music while studying or to study in a quiet place. Complete the two-way frequency table. What percent of 10th graders listen to music while studying?

grade	music	quiet	total
9	28	12	
10	9	31	
total			

Percent of 10th graders who listen to music while studying: _____

30. Match each pair of points to the slope of the line that passes through them.

(3, 18) and (−2, 8) $\frac{1}{2}$

(2, −5) and (−4, 7)   2

(12, −3) and (−12, 9) $-\frac{1}{2}$

(−4, −2) and (12, 6)   −2

Short Response

31. The ages of the members of a chess club are 13, 15, 22, 23, 35, 38, 49, and 56. A new member who is 48 years old joins the club. In general, describe how this will affect the mean, median, mode, and range of the ages of the club.

32. What is the factored form of $6x^4 - 16x^3 - 6x^2$? Show or explain your work.

33. The measure of angle A of an obtuse triangle is three times the measure of angle B, while the measure of angle C is one-half times the measure of angle B. What are the degree measures of the three angles? Show or explain your work.

34. What are the zeros of the function $f(x) = 2x^2 - 6x + 4$? Show or explain your work.

Extended Response

35. Dimitri has a combination of 30 nickels and dimes for a total of $2.10.

Part A

Write a system of equations you could use to determine the number of each type of coin Dimitri has.

Part B

How many of each type of coin does Dimitri have? Show or explain your work.

36. a. Graph the piecewise-defined function.

$$f(x) = \begin{cases} 2x - 2, \text{ if } x < -2 \\ 1.5x, \text{ if } -2 \leq x < 4 \\ 2, \text{ if } x > 4 \end{cases}$$

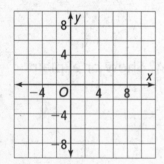

b. What are the domain and range of the function?

c. Over which intervals is the function increasing? Decreasing?

Practice Test Form A

Performance Task: Projectile Motion

Complete this performance task in the space provided. Fully answer all parts of the performance task with detailed responses. You should provide sound mathematical reasoning to support your work.

Suppose an object is thrown at an angle of 45° with respect to horizontal. The object will have height y ft after it has traveled a horizontal distance of x ft, where the relationship between x and y is described by the equation

$$y = -\frac{g}{v^2}x^2 + x + y_0.$$

In this equation, v is the object's initial speed (in feet per second), y_0 is the object's initial height (in feet), and $g \approx 32$ ft/s^2 is the acceleration due to gravity.

Task Description

Sarah throws a baseball toward her friend Felipe at an angle of 45° with respect to horizontal. Felipe is standing 90 ft away from Sarah, holding his glove 5 ft above the ground, ready to catch the ball. At what initial height, and with what initial speed, should Sarah throw the ball so that Felipe can catch it without moving his glove?

a. Suppose Sarah throws the baseball with an initial height of 5 ft and an initial speed of 60 ft/s. Write and graph an equation that represents the ball's path. Does the ball land in Felipe's glove? Explain.

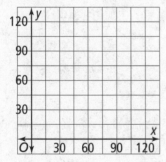

b. If your friend catches the ball, what point must lie on the graph of the ball's path? (Assume you are standing at the point (0, 0).) Explain your reasoning.

c. Use your answer to part (b) to write an equation that describes the initial heights and initial speeds for which your friend catches the ball. Explain why there is more than one initial height and initial speed that work.

d. Find an initial height and an initial speed for which your friend catches the ball. How can you check your answer?

Practice Test Form B

Part I: Calculator NOT Permitted

1. Which of the following are irrational numbers? Select all that apply.

   (A) $\sqrt{11}$

   (B) $\sqrt{7}$

   (C) $\sqrt{16}$

   (D) -13

   (E) $\frac{3}{8}$

2. Rewrite $\frac{(3)^4(5)^{-3}}{(3)^{-7}(5)^5}$ using positive exponents.

   (A) $\frac{3^{11}}{5^8}$

   (B) $\frac{3^3}{5^2}$

   (C) $\frac{5^2}{3^3}$

   (D) $\frac{5^8}{3^{11}}$

3. What is the solution to the equation $|3x - 3| + 3 = 9$? Select all that apply.

   (A) -3

   (B) -1

   (C) 3

   (D) 4

   (E) 6

4. Which equation represents a line perpendicular to a line that passes through the points $(-2, -2)$ and $(2, 4)$?

   (A) $y = -\frac{2}{3}x - 1$

   (B) $y = -\frac{3}{2}x - 1$

   (C) $y = \frac{2}{3}x - 1$

   (D) $y = \frac{3}{2}x - 1$

5. Mai works part-time to earn money for a trip. The amount she saves after working x hours is given by the equation $y = 12.5x + 20$. How much does Mai earn per hour?

6. Simplify $(2x^2y^2)^4$.

   (A) $2x^6y^6$

   (B) $8x^8y^8$

   (C) $16x^8y^8$

   (D) $32x^6y^6$

7. Identify the piecewise-defined function that has the same graph as the function $f(x) = |3x + 5|$.

Ⓐ $g(x) = \begin{cases} 3x + 5, & \text{if } x \geq 0 \\ -3x - 5, & \text{if } x < 0 \end{cases}$

Ⓑ $g(x) = \begin{cases} -3x - 5, & \text{if } x \geq -\frac{3}{5} \\ 3x + 5, & \text{if } x < -\frac{3}{5} \end{cases}$

Ⓒ $g(x) = \begin{cases} 3x + 5, & \text{if } x \geq -\frac{5}{3} \\ -3x - 5, & \text{if } x < -\frac{5}{3} \end{cases}$

Ⓓ $g(x) = \begin{cases} 3x + 5, & \text{if } x \geq 0 \\ -3x - 5, & \text{if } x < 0 \end{cases}$

8. What type of function is $f(x) = 2x^2 - 5x - 3$?

Ⓐ exponential

Ⓑ linear

Ⓒ quadratic

Ⓓ none of the above

9. A student has scores of 87, 78, 94, and 84. What score must the student earn on the fifth test in order to have an average score of 87?

10. What is an equation for the graph?

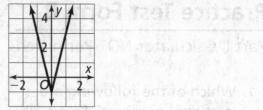

Ⓐ $y = -|2x - 4|$

Ⓑ $y = |2x - 4|$

Ⓒ $y = 4|x - 1|$

Ⓓ $y = |4x| - 1$

11. Which of the following is the best estimate of an equation of a line of best fit for the scatter plot below?

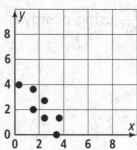

Ⓐ $y = x + 4$

Ⓑ $y = -x + 4$

Ⓒ $y = x + 3$

Ⓓ $y = -x + 3$

12. Order the numbers from least to greatest.

$\frac{3}{2}, -\sqrt{7}, -2, -\sqrt{9}, \frac{2}{3}, 1$

Short Response

13. Find the mean and median for the data shown in the dot plot to the nearest hundredth. Explain why they are different.

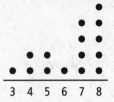

14. The area of a rectangle is $2x^2 - 2x - 12$. The width is $x - 3$. What is the length?

15. Graph the inequality $3x + 2y < 3$.

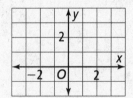

16. Graph the function $f(x) = x^2 + 4x + 2$.

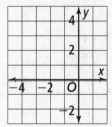

Extended Response

17. A ball is thrown directly upward from a height of 25 feet with an initial velocity of 96 feet per second. The equation $h = -16t^2 + 96t + 25$ gives the height h after t seconds.

Part A

How long does it take for the ball to reach its maximum height? Show or explain your work.

Part B

What is the maximum height of the ball? Show or explain your work.

18. Refer to the table below.

x	1	1.5	2	2.5	3	3.5	4
y	2	2.5	3.5	3	4.5	4	5

Part A

Make a scatter plot of the data.

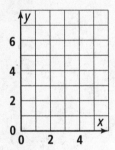

Part B

Estimate an equation of a line of best fit.

Practice Test Form B

Part II: Calculator Permitted

19. The length of the hypotenuse of a right triangle is 40 cm. One of the legs measures 24 cm. What is the length of the other leg?

Ⓐ 20 cm

Ⓑ 28 cm

Ⓒ 32 cm

Ⓓ 36 cm

20. Use the Quadratic Formula to solve the equation $3x^2 + 5x - 5 = -1$. Which of the following are solutions of the equation to the nearest hundredth? Select all that apply.

Ⓐ −2.48

Ⓑ −2.37

Ⓒ −2.26

Ⓓ 0.59

Ⓔ 0.70

Ⓕ 0.81

21. How can you describe the graph of $y = 2x - 4$ as a transformation of the graph of $y = 2x$?

Ⓐ translation 4 units down

Ⓑ translation 4 unlts up

Ⓒ translation 4 units left

Ⓓ translation 4 units right

22. Graph the solution to the inequality $-4x - 3 < 13$.

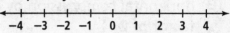

23. Which function does the table represent?

x	−2	−1	0	1	2
y	4	3	2	1	0

Ⓐ $y = 2x$

Ⓑ $y = -2x$

Ⓒ $y = x + 2$

Ⓓ $y = -x + 2$

24. You deposit $325 in an account that pays 5% interest compounded quarterly. Use the formula $A = P\left(1 + \frac{r}{n}\right)^{nt}$ to determine how much you will have in the account after 5 years.

25. Which of the following describes the graph of the function $y = \sqrt[3]{2x}$ as a transformation of the graph of the parent function $y = \sqrt[3]{x}$?

Ⓐ translation 2 units right

Ⓑ horizontal compression by a factor of 2

Ⓒ horizontal stretch by a factor of 2

Ⓓ reflection across the line with equation $x = 2$

26. What is the solution of the system?
$y = 2x - 3$
$y = x + 4$

27. Which of the following is an equation for the transformation of the graph of the parent function $y = \sqrt{x}$ shown below?

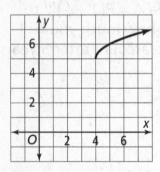

Ⓐ $y = \sqrt{x + 4} - 5$

Ⓑ $y = \sqrt{x - 4} + 5$

Ⓒ $y = \sqrt{x - 5} + 4$

Ⓓ $y = \sqrt{x + 5} - 4$

28. The formula for the volume of a cylinder in cubic feet is $V = \pi r^2 h$ where r is the radius of the base, in feet, and h is the height, in feet. A cylinder has a volume of 648π ft^3. Its height is 18 feet. What is its diameter?

29. Students in 9th and 10th grade were asked whether they preferred to listen to music while studying or to study in a quiet place. Complete the two-way frequency table. What percent of students who listen to music while studying are in 9th grade?

grade	music	quiet	total
9	16	49	
10	64	21	
total			

Percent of students who listen to music while studying who are in 9th grade: _____

30. Match each pair of points to the slope of the line that passes through them.

(7, 12) and (−5, 8) $\frac{1}{3}$

(1, −3) and (−2, 6)   3

(15, −15) and (−12, −6) $-\frac{1}{3}$

(−7, −2) and (−5, 4)   −3

Short Response

31. The ages of the members of a sailing club are 18, 19, 24, 28, 33, 37, 42, and 46. A new member who is 42 years old joins the club. In general, describe how this will affect the mean, median, mode, and range of the ages of the club.

32. What is the factored form of $8x^4 - 4x^3 - 24x^2$? Show or explain your work.

33. The measure of angle A of an obtuse triangle is two times the measure of angle B, while the measure of angle C is 30° greater than the measure of angle B. What are the degree measures of the three angles? Show or explain your work.

34. What are the zeros of the function $f(x) = 4x^2 - 10x - 6$? Show or explain your work.

Extended Response

35. Dalia has a combination of 24 nickels and quarters for a total of $2.60.

Part A

Write a system of equations you could use to determine the number of each type of coin Dalia has.

Part B

How many of each type of coin does Dalia have? Show or explain your work.

36. a. Graph the piecewise-defined function.

$$f(x) = \begin{cases} \frac{3}{2}x - 4, \text{ if, } x < 0 \\ \frac{1}{3}x - 4, \text{ if } 0 \leq x < 6 \\ 2x - 10, \text{ if } x > 6 \end{cases}$$

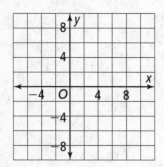

b. What are the domain and range of the function?

c. Over which intervals is the function increasing? Decreasing?

Practice Test Form B

Performance Task: Expanding a Parking Lot

Complete this performance task in the space provided. Fully answer all parts of the performance task with detailed responses. You should provide sound mathematical reasoning to support your work.

A high school has a rectangular parking lot that measures 400 ft long by 250 ft wide. The school board wants to double the area of the lot by increasing both its length and width by the same amount, x ft. The board also wants to build a fence around the new lot. The cost to expand the lot is estimated to be $1.50 per square foot of new space. The fence will cost $20 per foot of fencing. Costs include labor and materials.

Task Description

Estimate the total cost of expanding and fencing in the lot.

a. Draw a diagram of the situation. Your diagram should show both the original parking lot and what the lot will look like after it has been expanded. Label all dimensions.

b. Write an equation that you can use to find x. Solve the equation for x, and explain your work. Round your answer to the nearest 10 ft.

c. What is the area of the new portion of the parking lot that needs to be built? What is the perimeter of the new parking lot? Explain.

d. What is the estimated cost of expanding and fencing in the new lot? Explain.

e. The school has only enough money to pay for half the estimated cost from part (d). The school board plans to raise the remaining funds by selling parking stickers for $150 to students and $250 to faculty. How many student stickers and how many faculty stickers must the school sell? Is there only one possible answer? Explain.

Practice Test Form C

Part I: Calculator NOT Permitted

1. Which of the following are irrational numbers? Select all that apply.

   Ⓐ $\frac{1}{7}$

   Ⓑ $\sqrt{3}$

   Ⓒ $\sqrt{15}$

   Ⓓ $\sqrt{25}$

   Ⓔ $\frac{2}{3}$

2. Rewrite $\frac{(3)^{-4}(7)^{-2}}{(3)^2(7)^{-5}}$ using positive exponents.

   Ⓐ $\frac{7^7}{3^6}$

   Ⓑ $\frac{7^3}{3^6}$

   Ⓒ $\frac{3^2}{7^3}$

   Ⓓ $\frac{3^6}{7^7}$

3. What is the solution to the equation $|2x - 3| - 4 = 3$? Select all that apply.

   Ⓐ -3

   Ⓑ -2

   Ⓒ 3

   Ⓓ 5

   Ⓔ 6

4. Which equation represents a line perpendicular to a line that passes through the points $(4, -1)$ and $(-4, 3)$?

   Ⓐ $y = \frac{1}{2}x - 1$

   Ⓑ $y = 2x - 1$

   Ⓒ $y = -\frac{1}{2}x - 1$

   Ⓓ $y = -2x - 1$

5. Miriam works part-time to earn money for a trip. The amount she saves after working x hours is given by the equation $y = 11.75x + 15$. How much does Miriam earn per hour?

6. Simplify $(6x^4y^6)^2$.

   Ⓐ $6x^6y^8$

   Ⓑ $12x^8y^{12}$

   Ⓒ $36x^8y^{12}$

   Ⓓ $36x^6y^8$

7. Identify the piecewise-defined function that has the same graph as the function $f(x) = |-x + 7|$.

Ⓐ $g(x) = \begin{cases} -x + 7, & \text{if } x \leq -7 \\ x - 7, & \text{if } x > -7 \end{cases}$

Ⓑ $(x) = \begin{cases} -x + 7, & \text{if } x \leq 7 \\ x - 7, & \text{if } x > 7 \end{cases}$

Ⓒ $g(x) = \begin{cases} -x + 7, & \text{if } x \geq 0 \\ x - 7, & \text{if } x < 0 \end{cases}$

Ⓓ $g(x) = \begin{cases} -x + 7, & \text{if } x \geq 7 \\ x - 7, & \text{if } x < 7 \end{cases}$

8. What type of function is $f(x) = 2^x$?

Ⓐ exponential

Ⓑ linear

Ⓒ quadratic

Ⓓ none of the above

9. A student has scores of 89, 98, 93, and 97. What score must the student earn on the fifth test in order to have an average score of 94?

10. What is an equation for the graph?

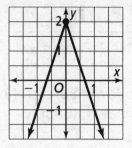

Ⓐ $y = -|3x| + 2$

Ⓑ $y = |3x + 2|$

Ⓒ $y = -3|x + 2|$

Ⓓ $y = |3x| + 2$

11. Which of the following is the best estimate of an equation of a line of best fit for the scatter plot below?

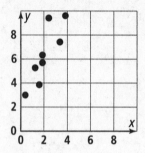

Ⓐ $y = x + 2$

Ⓑ $y = -x + 2$

Ⓒ $y = 2x + 2$

Ⓓ $y = -2x + 2$

12. Order the numbers from least to greatest.

$$-\frac{1}{4}, -1, \sqrt{3}, -\sqrt{8}, \frac{1}{2}, 3$$

Short Response

13. Find the mean and median for the data shown in the dot plot to the nearest hundredth. Explain why they are different.

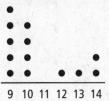

9 10 11 12 13 14

14. The area of a rectangle is $12x^2 + x - 6$. The width is $3x - 2$. What is the length?

15. Graph the inequality $2x + 4y < 4$.

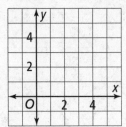

16. Graph the function $f(x) = x^2 - 4x + 5$.

Extended Response

17. A ball is thrown directly upward from a height of 2 feet with an initial velocity of 16 feet per second. The equation $h = -16t^2 + 16t + 2$ gives the height h after t seconds.

Part A

How long does it take for the ball to reach its maximum height? Show or explain your work.

Part B

What is the maximum height of the ball? Show or explain your work.

18. Refer to the table below.

x	1	1.5	2	2.5	3	3.5	4
y	5	4.5	3.5	4	2.5	3	2

Part A

Make a scatter plot of the data.

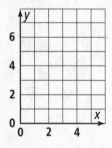

Part B

Estimate an equation of a line of best fit.

Practice Test Form C

Part II: Calculator Permitted

19. The length of the hypotenuse of a right triangle is 25 cm. One of the legs measures 20 cm. What is the length of the other leg?

    (A) 10 cm

    (B) 15 cm

    (C) 20 cm

    (D) 22 cm

20. Use the Quadratic Formula to solve the equation $5x^2 - 18x + 9 = -3$. Which of the following are solutions of the equation to the nearest hundredth? Select all that apply.

    (A) 0.37

    (B) 0.6

    (C) 0.88

    (D) 2.72

    (E) 3

    (F) 3.23

21. How can you describe the graph of $y = 3x + 3$ as a transformation of the graph of $y = 3x$?

    (A) translation 3 units left

    (B) translation 3 units right

    (C) translation 3 units down

    (D) translation 3 units up

22. Graph the solution to the inequality $-2x + 5 < 1$.

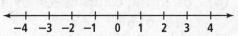

23. Which function does the table represent?

x	-2	-1	0	1	2
y	8	4	0	-4	-8

    (A) $y = 4x$

    (B) $y = -4x$

    (C) $y = x + 4$

    (D) $y = -x + -4$

24. You deposit $500 in an account that pays 2% interest compounded monthly. Use the formula $A = P\left(1 + \frac{r}{n}\right)^{nt}$ to determine how much you will have in the account after 5 years.

25. Which of the following describes the graph of the function $y = \sqrt[3]{\frac{x}{6}}$ as a transformation of the graph of the parent function $y = \sqrt[3]{x}$?

Ⓐ translation 6 units left

Ⓑ horizontal compression by a factor of 6

Ⓒ horizontal stretch by a factor of 6

Ⓓ reflection across the line with equation $x = 6$

26. What is the solution of the system?
$y = -2x - 4$
$y = -4x - 2$

27. Which of the following is an equation for the transformation of the graph of the parent function $y = \sqrt{x}$ shown below?

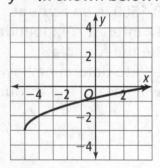

Ⓐ $y = \sqrt{x + 5} - 3$

Ⓑ $y = \sqrt{x - 3} + 5$

Ⓒ $y = \sqrt{x - 5} + 3$

Ⓓ $y = \sqrt{x + 3} + 5$

28. The formula for the volume of a cylinder in cubic feet is $V = \pi r^2 h$ where r is the radius of the base, in feet, and h is the height, in feet. A cylinder has a volume of $1{,}078\pi$ ft^3. Its height is 22 feet. What is its diameter?

29. Students in 9th and 10th grade were asked whether they preferred to listen to music while studying or to study in a quiet place. Complete the two-way frequency table. What percent of the students listen to music while studying?

grade	music	quiet	total
9	34	26	
10	11	49	
total			

Percent of students who listen to music while studying: _____

30. Match each pair of points to the slope of the line that passes through them.

(3, 1) and (5, −7) $\frac{1}{4}$

(10, 14) and (−2, 11)   4

(−11, 9) and (−12, 5) $-\frac{1}{4}$

(−2, 7) and (−10, 9)   −4

Short Response

31. The ages of the members of a beach clean-up club are 16, 19, 22, 25, 31, 33, 38, and 42. A new member who is 19 years old joins the club. In general, describe how this will affect the mean, median, mode, and range of the ages of the club.

32. What is the factored form of $8x^5 - 26x^4 + 6x^3$? Show or explain your work.

33. The measure of angle A of an obtuse triangle is two times the measure of angle B, while the measure of angle C is 28° less than the measure of angle B. What are the degree measures of the three angles? Show or explain your work.

34. What are the zeros of the function $f(x) = 9x^2 + 15x - 6$? Show or explain your work.

Extended Response

35. Dakota has a combination of 18 dimes and quarters for a total of $2.70.

Part A

Write a system of equations you could use to determine the number of each type of coin Dakota has.

Part B

How many of each type of coin does Dakota have? Show or explain your work.

36. a. Graph the piecewise-defined function.

$$f(x) = \begin{cases} 4x + 7, \text{ if } x < -2 \\ -x, \text{ if } -2 < x \leq 2 \\ 1, \text{ if } x > 2 \end{cases}$$

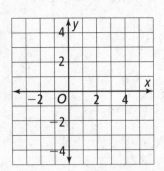

b. What are the domain and range of the function?

c. Over which intervals is the function increasing? Decreasing?

Practice Test Form C

Performance Task: Choosing a Media-Rental Plan

Complete this performance task in the space provided. Fully answer all parts of the performance task with detailed responses. You should provide sound mathematical reasoning to support your work.

Kayden is considering three different ways to rent movies and video games.

Plan A: Rent movie and game disks from a kiosk in a nearby grocery store for $2.00 each. The selection is limited, especially for video games.

Plan B: Stream unlimited movies and games to any devices for $20 per month. The selection is good.

Plan C: Rent movie and game disks by mail for a $10 monthly fee plus $2.50 per disk. The selection is outstanding.

Task Description

Choose the media-rental plan that you think is best for Kayden. Consider the cost of each plan, the selection offered, and convenience.

a. Write functions $A(x)$, $B(x)$, and $C(x)$, that give the cost to rent x movie or game disks per month for Plans A, B, and C, respectively. Graph the functions, and explain your reasoning.

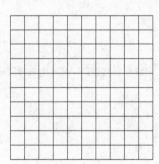

b. If you consider only cost, under what conditions does it make sense for Kayden to choose Plan B over Plan A? Why?

c. If you consider only cost, under what conditions does it make sense for Kayden to choose Plan C over Plan B? Why?

d. Show that Plan A is always more cost-effective than Plan C. Does that mean that Plan A is a better choice than Plan C for everyone? Explain.

e. Which movie plan would you recommend for Kayden? Justify your answer.

Name _____

Progress Monitoring for Algebra 1 Practice Tests

Item	Objective	Test 1 ✓ or X	Test 2 ✓ or X	Test 3 ✓ or X	Lesson
1	Identify irrational numbers.				1-1
2	Use exponents in equivalent expressions.				6-1
3	Solve equations with absolute value.				1-7
4	Find the equation for a parallel line.				2-4
5	Interpret the meaning of a rate.				2-1, 2-2
6	Simplify expressions with exponents.				6-1
7	Identify the piecewise-function equivalent to an absolute value function				5-2
8	Determine the type of function from the equation.				8-5
9	Use the mean to find a missing data value.				11-2
10	Match an absolute value function to its graph.				5-1
11	Find a line of best fit.				3-5

Item	Objective	Test 1 ✓ or X	Test 2 ✓ or X	Test 3 ✓ or X	Lesson
12	Order rational and irrational numbers.				1-1
13	Analyze a dot plot.				11-3
14	Find the missing factor for a quadratic expression.				7-6
15	Graph an algebraic inequality in two variables.				4-4
16	Graph a quadratic function.				8-1, 8-3
17	Use a quadratic function to solve a problem.				8-3
18	Create a scatterplot and find a line of best fit.				3-5, 3-6
19	Find the missing side length of a right triangle.				9-4
20	Use the Quadratic Formula to solve an equation.				9-6
21	Determine how a linear equation is translated from its parent.				3-3
22	Graph an inequality in one variable.				1-6
23	Find a function from a table.				3-2

Item	Objective	Test 1 ✓ or ✗	Test 2 ✓ or ✗	Test 3 ✓ or ✗	Lesson
24	Calculate compound interest.				6-3
25	Describe a transformation of a cube root graph given its equation.				10-2, 10-4
26	Solve a system of linear equations.				4-2, 4-3
27	Identify the equation of a transformation of a square root function given its graph.				10-1, 10-3
28	Find the diameter of a cylinder given volume and height.				1-4
29	Complete and use a two-way frequency table.				11-5
30	Find the slope of a line given two points.				2-1
31	Describe how a change to the data affects statistical measures.				11-1
32	Factor a polynomial expression.				7-6
33	Use algebra to find the angle measures of a triangle.				1-2
34	Find the zeros of a quadratic function.				8-1

Item	Objective	Test 1 ✓ or ✗	Test 2 ✓ or ✗	Test 3 ✓ or ✗	Lesson
35	Write and solve a system of equations to solve a real-world problem.				4-2, 4-3
36	Graph a piecewise-defined function and describe key features.				5-2
PT-A	Analyze projectile motion				8-4
PT-B	Use polynomials to model area and costs.				7-1, 7-2
PT-C	Compare linear functions.				2-1, 2-2

Name _____

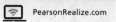

Table 1 Measures

	United States Customary	Metric
Length	12 inches (in.) = 1 foot (ft) 36 in. = 1 yard (yd) 3 ft = 1 yd 5,280 ft = 1 mile (mi) 1,760 yd = 1 mi	10 mm = 1 centimeter (cm) 100 cm = 1 meter (m) 1,000 mm = 1 m 1,000 m = 1 kilometer (km)
Capacity	8 (fl oz) = 1 cup (c) 2 c = 1 pint (pt) 2 pt = 1 quart (qt) 4 qt = 1 gallon (gal)	1,000 (mL) = 1 liter (L) 1,000 L = 1 kiloliter (kL)
Weight or Mass	16 ounces (oz) = 1 pound (lb) 2,000 lb = 1 ton (t)	1,000 (mg) = 1 gram (g) 1,000 g = 1 kilogram (kg) 1,000 kg = 1 metric ton

	Customary Units and Metric Units
Length	1 in. = 2.54 cm 1 mi ≈ 1.61 km 1 ft ≈ 0.305 m
Capacity	1 qt ≈ 0.946 L
Weight or Mass	1 oz ≈ 28.4 g 1 lb ≈ 0.454 kg

Time	
60 seconds (s) = 1 (min) 60 min = 1 hour (h) 24 h = 1 day (d) 7 d = 1 (wk)	4 weeks = 1 month (mo) 365 d = 1 year (yr) 52 wk = 1 year 12 mo = 1 yr

Formulas of Geometry

Here are some perimeter, area, and volume formulas.	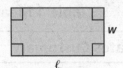 $P = 2l + 2w$ $A = lw$ **Rectangle**	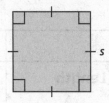 $P = 4s$ $A = s^2$ **Square**
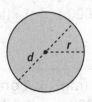 $C = 2\pi r$ or $C = \pi d$ $A = \pi r^2$ **Circle**	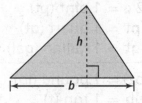 $A = \frac{1}{2}bh$ **Triangle**	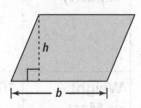 $A = bh$ **Parallelogram**
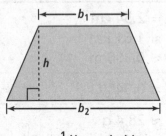 $A = \frac{1}{2}(b_1 + b_2)h$ **Trapezoid**	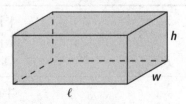 $V = Bh$ $V = lwh$ **Right Prism**	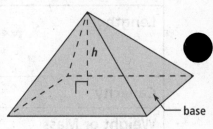 $V = \frac{1}{3}Bh$ **Right Pyramid**
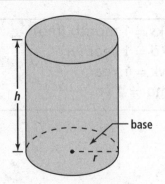 $V = Bh$ $V = \pi r^2 h$ **Right Cylinder**	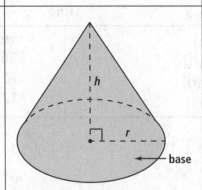 $V = \frac{1}{3}Bh$ $V = \frac{1}{3}\pi r^2 h$ **Right Cone**	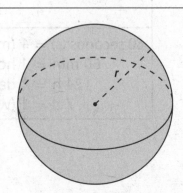 $V = \frac{4}{3}\pi r^3$ **Sphere**